To Dear Rosa

A very belated
21ˢᵗ birthday present
for you!

I am sure you will spend
many happy hours playing
the wonderful music in
this book.

With much love

Malcolm xxx

JOHANNES BRAHMS

Complete Shorter Works for Solo Piano

EDITED BY

EUSEBIUS MANDYCZEWSKI

THE VIENNA GESELLSCHAFT DER MUSIKFREUNDE EDITION

Dover Publications, Inc., New York

This Dover edition, first published in 1971, is an unabridged
republication of Volume (*Band*) 14, entitled *Kleinere Klavierwerke*, of
the collection *Johannes Brahms; Sämtliche Werke; Ausgabe der
Gesellschaft der Musikfreunde in Wien*, originally published by Breitkopf
& Härtel, Leipzig (n.d.; Editor's Preface to Volume 14 dated
Spring, 1927).
The English translation of the Editor's Preface (*Revisionsbericht*) and
of the table of contents was prepared specially for this Dover edition.

International Standard Book Number: 0-486-22651-4
Library of Congress Catalog Card Number: 70-116828

Manufactured in the United States of America
Dover Publications, Inc.
31 East 2nd Street, Mineola, N.Y. 11501

CONTENTS

EDITOR'S PREFACE

SCHERZO FOR PIANO, Op. 4.

BASIC TEXTS FOR THE PRESENT EDITION:

1. Brahms's original manuscript, in the collection of Breitkopf & Härtel, Leipzig. Four oblong leaves of sixteen-staff piano music paper, with the heading: "Scherzo für das Pianoforte von Joh⁵ Brahms. op. 4." No date of composition.
2. The composer's personal copy of the first edition, in the collection of the Gesellschaft der Musikfreunde, Vienna. This edition was published in 1854 with the title: "Scherzo Es moll für das Pianoforte componirt und seinem Freunde Ernst Ferdinand Wenzel zugeeignet von Johannes Brahms. op. 4. Eigenthum der Verleger. Leipzig, bei Breitkopf & Härtel." Publication number 8836.

COMMENTS:

The manuscript shows divisions into plates, so that it was clearly used as engraving copy for the first edition. Accordingly the two basic texts agree almost completely. The first edition was authoritative for us. The *staccato*, which is so important in this piece, is indicated in the manuscript now with dashes now with dots, without real consistency. The first edition, flawlessly correct and thus surely proofread carefully by the composer, does not show this different treatment. Originally the manuscript (page 1) gave the first note of the left hand as ♮d¹, and similarly two and four measures later. This was already changed in the manuscript. The tempo changes at the end, page 12, lines 3, 4 and 6, are also still missing in the manuscript.

BALLADES FOR PIANO, Op. 10.

BASIC TEXTS FOR THE PRESENT EDITION:

1. A copy, which Brahms read and corrected in many places, in the collection of Breitkopf & Härtel, Leipzig, with the autograph title: "Balladen und ein Intermezzo für Pianoforte Julius O. Grimm gewidmet von Johannes Brahms. opus 10." Brahms later crossed out the second, third and fourth words. Plate divisions show that this copy was used as engraving copy for the first edition.
2. The composer's personal copy of the first edition, in the collection of the Gesellschaft der Musikfreunde, Vienna. This edition was published in 1856 with the title: "Balladen für das Pianoforte Julius O. Grimm gewidmet von Johannes Brahms. op. 10. Eigenthum der Verleger. Leipzig, bei Breitkopf & Härtel." Publication number 9226.

COMMENT:

In his personal copy Brahms corrected minor engraving errors.

In both basic texts, however, he is not very precise in the use of slurs. He leaves a great deal to the discretion of the performer as being self-evident. We shall follow him in this.

WALTZES FOR PIANO, Op. 39.

BASIC TEXT FOR THE PRESENT EDITION:

The composer's personal copy of the first edition, in the collection of the Gesellschaft der Musikfreunde, Vienna. This edition appeared in 1867 with the title: "Dr. Eduard Hanslick zugeeignet. Walzer für das Pianoforte componirt von Johannes Brahms. op. 39. Zu zwei Händen. Zu vier Händen. Leichte Ausgabe zu zwei Händen. Eigenthum des Verlegers für alle Länder. Leipzig und Winterthur, J. Rieter-Biedermann." Publication numbers 470, 524, 525.

COMMENT:

The perfectly correct first edition was not altered in the personal copy and was able to be considered authoritative.

EIGHT PIECES, Op. 76.

BASIC TEXT FOR THE PRESENT EDITION:

The composer's personal copy of the first edition, in the collection of the Gesellschaft der Musikfreunde, Vienna. This edition appeared with the title: "Clavierstücke von Johannes Brahms. Op. 76. Erstes Heft: No. 1. Capriccio, Fis moll. No. 2. Capriccio, H. moll. No. 3. Intermezzo, As dur. No. 4. Intermezzo, B dur. Zweites Heft: No. 5. Capriccio, Cis moll. No. 6. Intermezzo, A dur. No. 7. Intermezzo, A moll. No. 8. Capriccio, C dur. Verlag und Eigenthum von N. Simrock in Berlin. 1879." Publication numbers 8090 and 8091.

COMMENTS:

The personal copy shows that Brahms gave his critical attention to this work even after its first publication. Isolated engraving errors are corrected, individual indications for the performer are added; for example: page (61)1, "(sotto)" and "(sopra)" (below, above); page (63)3, the fingering in measure 5; page (75)15, the "m.d." and "d." in measures 5 to 8. Two passages were really altered. On page 8(68), last line, measures 1 and 2, the right hand originally had:

On page 24(84), line 3, measures 4 and 5 originally formed one 3/2 measure:

We might also mention as especially characteristic that on page 14(74), below, Brahms originally let the *string*. – – – continue up to the *p*, and later in this personal copy shortened it by one measure as clearly as possible.

––––––

TWO RHAPSODIES, Op. 79.

BASIC TEXT FOR THE PRESENT EDITION:

The composer's personal copy of the first edition, in the collection of the Gesellschaft der Musikfreunde, Vienna. This edition was published with the title: "Frau Elisabeth von Herzogenberg gewidmet. Zwei Rhapsodien für das Pianoforte von Johannes Brahms. Op. 79. Verlag und Eigenthum von N. Simrock in Berlin. 1880." Publication number 8166.

COMMENT:

In his personal copy Brahms made an attempt to introduce a small alteration toward the end of the first rhapsody, but changed his mind, apparently at once. This clearly shows, however, that he was deeply concerned with his work even after publication. The first edition is flawless and was able to be republished faithfully.

––––––

FANTASIES FOR PIANO, Op. 116.

BASIC TEXT FOR THE PRESENT EDITION:

The composer's personal copy of the first edition, in the collection of the Gesellschaft der Musikfreunde, Vienna. This edition was published with the title: "Fantasien für Pianoforte von Johannes Brahms. op. 116, Erstes Heft: No. 1. Capriccio. No. 2 Intermezzo. No. 3. Capriccio. Zweites Heft: No. 4. Intermezzo. No. 5. Intermezzo. No. 6. Intermezzo. No. 7. Capriccio. Verlag und Eigenthum für alle Länder von N. Simrock in Berlin. 1892." Publication numbers 9874 and 9875.

COMMENT:

The extremely correct and magnificently engraved first edition, to which Brahms made no later additions, was our authority. At most we might add that No. 4 was originally called "Notturno" and No. 7 "Intermezzo."

––––––

THREE INTERMEZZI FOR PIANO, Op. 117.

BASIC TEXTS FOR THE PRESENT EDITION:

1. The composer's original manuscript, in the collection of the Gesellschaft der Musikfreunde, Vienna. Six vertical leaves of twelve-staff piano music paper with no heading, signature or date.

2. The composer's personal copy of the first edition, in the same collection. This edition was published with the title: "Drei Intermezzi für Pianoforte von Johannes Brahms. Op. 117. No. 1. No. 2. No. 3. Verlag und Eigenthum für alle Länder von N. Simrock in Berlin. 1892." Publication number 9876.

COMMENTS:

In his personal copy Brahms later corrected a few unimportant engraving errors. Otherwise the first edition is flawless and was our authority. It also agrees completely with the manuscript (even though this was not engraving copy), except for the following minor items: On page 4(132), the tempo indication in the manuscript is simply "Andante con moto." On page (133)5, precisely in the middle of measure 3, before the beginning of the *p*, a "breath pause," separating the two parts of the work (B-flat minor and D-flat major), is indicated in both systems by free-standing ⌢ as a result of the *rit*. – – –. On page 6(134), measure 1, an *f* is prescribed for the last note of the right hand as a result of the <, followed immediately by the *p* of the next measure. The manuscript's c^2 for the antepenultimate note of the right hand in line 4, measure 2, of page 6(134) is surely a mere slip of the pen; the same holds for page (135)7, next-to-last measure, where the first note of the left hand is missing one leger line in the manuscript and appears as $D\text{-flat}_1$. In the following, penultimate, measure, the manuscript does not show the notes for the left hand; but this is no writing error. On page (139)11, line 3, measure 3, the tied notes for the thumb of the left hand are *e* (not *d*) in the manuscript. The passage on page 12(140), measures 9–11, was originally written like measures 9 and 10 on page (137)9; when the piece was completed, Brahms at first changed it to this:

then, still in the manuscript, to the way it was printed.

––––––

PIANO PIECES, Opp. 118 and 119.

BASIC TEXT FOR THE PRESENT EDITION:

The composer's personal copy of the first edition, in the collection of the Gesellschaft der Musikfreunde, Vienna. This edition was published with the title: "Clavierstücke von Johannes Brahms. op. 118. No. 1. Intermezzo, A moll. No. 2. Intermezzo, A dur. No. 3. Ballade, G moll. No. 4. Intermezzo, F moll. No. 5. Romanze, F dur. No. 6. Intermezzo, Es moll. op. 119. No. 1. Intermezzo, H moll. No. 2. Intermezzo, E moll. No. 3. Intermezzo, C dur. No. 4. Rhapsodie, Es dur. Verlag und Eigenthum für alle Länder von N. Simrock in Berlin. 1893." Two brochure volumes. Publication numbers 10054 and 10055.

COMMENT:

The personal copy shows no later alterations by Brahms; its great accuracy made it our authority. We differ here from the two brochure volumes in giving the number of pieces in our titles.

Vienna   EUSEBIUS MANDYCZEWSKI
Spring, 1927

REVISIONSBERICHT

SCHERZO FÜR DAS PIANOFORTE. Op. 4.

VORLAGEN:

1. Die Original-Handschrift von Brahms im Besitz von Breitkopf & Härtel in Leipzig. Vier Blätter sechzehnlinigen Notenpapiers für Klavier in Querformat, überschrieben »Scherzo für das Pianoforte von Johs Brahms. op. 4.« Ohne Kompositionsdatum.

2. Des Komponisten Handexemplar der ersten Ausgabe im Besitz der Gesellschaft der Musikfreunde in Wien. Diese Ausgabe erschien 1854 unter dem Titel »Scherzo Es moll für das Pianoforte componirt und seinem Freunde Ernst Ferdinand Wenzel zugeeignet von Johannes Brahms. op. 4. Eigenthum der Verleger. Leipzig, bei Breitkopf & Härtel.« Verlagsnummer 8836.

BEMERKUNGEN:

Die Handschrift weist Platteneintheilung auf, aus der ersichtlich ist, daß sie für die erste Ausgabe als Stichvorlage gedient hat. Dementsprechend stimmen die beiden Vorlagen auch fast vollständig überein. Für uns war die erste Ausgabe maßgebend. Das in diesem Stück so wichtige staccato ist in der Handschrift bald mit Strichen, bald mit Punkten bezeichnet, ohne eigentliche Folgerichtigkeit. Die tadellos korrekte, also wohl vom Komponisten sorgfältig durchgesehene erste Ausgabe kennt auch diesen Unterschied nicht. Ursprünglich war in der Handschrift (Seite 1) die erste Note der linken Hand ♮d', und ebenso nach zwei und nach vier Takten. Das ist schon in der Handschrift geändert. Die Tempoänderungen am Schluß, Seite 12, Zeile 3, 4 und 6 fehlen auch noch in der Handschrift.

BALLADEN FÜR PIANOFORTE. Op. 10.

VORLAGEN:

1. Eine von Brahms durchgesehene und vielfach verbesserte Abschrift im Besitz von Breitkopf & Härtel in Leipzig mit dem autographen Titel »Balladen und ein Intermezzo für Pianoforte Julius O. Grimm gewidmet von Johannes Brahms. opus 10.« Das 2., 3. und 4. Wort von Brahms nachträglich gestrichen. Plattenzeichen zeigen, daß diese Abschrift Stichvorlage war für die erste Ausgabe.

2. Des Komponisten Handexemplar der ersten Ausgabe im Besitz der Gesellschaft der Musikfreunde in Wien. Diese Ausgabe erschien 1856 unter dem Titel »Balladen für das Pianoforte Julius O. Grimm gewidmet von Johannes Brahms. op. 10. Eigenthum der Verleger. Leipzig, bei Breitkopf & Härtel.« Verlagsnummer 9226.

BEMERKUNG:

Im Handexemplar hat Brahms kleine Stichfehler korrigiert. In der Verwendung der legato-Bogen zeigt er sich aber in beiden Vorlagen nicht sehr genau. Gar manches darin überläßt er als selbstverständlich dem Spieler. Wir wollen es auch so halten.

WALZER FÜR PIANOFORTE. Op. 39.

VORLAGE:

Des Komponisten Handexemplar der ersten Ausgabe im Besitz der Gesellschaft der Musikfreunde in Wien. Diese Ausgabe erschien 1867 unter dem Titel »Dr. Eduard Hanslick zugeeignet. Walzer für das Pianoforte componirt von Johannes Brahms. op. 39. Zu zwei Händen. Zu vier Händen. Leichte Ausgabe zu zwei Händen. Eigenthum des Verlegers für alle Länder. Leipzig und Winterthur, J. Rieter-Biedermann.« Verlagsnummern 470, 524, 525.

BEMERKUNG:

Die durchaus korrekte erste Ausgabe erfuhr auch im Handexemplar keine Veränderung und konnte als maßgebend gelten.

ACHT KLAVIERSTÜCKE. Op. 76.

VORLAGE:

Des Komponisten Handexemplar der ersten Ausgabe im Besitz der Gesellschaft der Musikfreunde in Wien. Diese Ausgabe erschien unter dem Titel »Clavierstücke von Johannes Brahms. Op. 76. Erstes Heft: No. 1. Capriccio, Fis moll. No. 2. Capriccio, H moll. No. 3. Intermezzo, As dur. No. 4. Intermezzo, B dur. Zweites Heft: No. 5. Capriccio, Cis moll. No. 6. Intermezzo, A dur. No. 7. Intermezzo, A moll. No. 8. Capriccio, C dur. Verlag und Eigenthum von N. Simrock in Berlin 1879.« Verlagsnummern 8090 und 8091.

BEMERKUNGEN:

Das Handexemplar zeigt, daß Brahms diesem Werke auch nach der ersten Veröffentlichung prüfende Aufmerksamkeit geschenkt hat. Vereinzelte Stichfehler werden korrigiert, für den Klavierspieler einzelne Hinweise gemacht, wie Seite (61) 1 (sotto) und (sopra), unten und oben; Seite (63) 3, Takt 5 der Fingersatz; Seite (75) 15, Takt 5 bis 8 das m. d. und d. Eigentliche Änderungen erfuhren zwei Stellen. Seite 8 (68), letzte Zeile, Takt 1 und 2 hatte die rechte Hand ursprünglich:

Seite 24 (84), Zeile 3, Takte 4 und 5 waren ursprünglich ein $^3/_2$-Takt:

Als besonders bezeichnend sei auch erwähnt, daß Brahms Seite 14 (74) unten das *string.* — — — ursprünglich bis zum *p* gehen ließ und nachträglich im Handexemplar möglichst deutlich um eine Taktlänge gekürzt hat.

ZWEI RHAPSODIEN. Op. 79.

VORLAGE:

Des Komponisten Handexemplar der ersten Ausgabe im Besitz der Gesellschaft der Musikfreunde in Wien. Diese Ausgabe erschien unter dem Titel »Frau Elisabeth von Herzogenberg gewidmet. Zwei Rhapsodien für das Pianoforte von Johannes Brahms. Op. 79. Verlag und Eigenthum von N. Simrock in Berlin. 1880.« Verlagsnummer 8166.

BEMERKUNG:

Im Handexemplar hat Brahms den Versuch gemacht, gegen Ende der ersten Rhapsodie eine kleine Änderung anzubringen, ist aber, offenbar gleich, auch davon abgekommen. Doch ersieht man daraus, daß er sich mit seinem Werk auch nach der Veröffentlichung noch eingehend beschäftigt hat. Die erste Ausgabe ist tadellos und war getreu wiederzugeben.

FANTASIEN FÜR PIANOFORTE. Op. 116.

VORLAGE:

Des Komponisten Handexemplar der ersten Ausgabe im Besitz der Gesellschaft der Musikfreunde in Wien. Diese Ausgabe erschien unter dem Titel »Fantasien für Pianoforte von Johannes Brahms. op. 116. Erstes Heft: No. 1. Capriccio. No. 2. Intermezzo. No. 3. Capriccio. Zweites Heft: No. 4. Intermezzo. No. 5. Intermezzo. No. 6. Intermezzo. No. 7. Capriccio. Verlag und Eigenthum für alle Länder von N. Simrock in Berlin. 1892.« Verlagsnummern 9874 und 9875.

BEMERKUNG:

Die äußerst korrekte und prachtvoll gestochene erste Ausgabe, der Brahms auch später nichts hinzuzufügen hatte, war uns maßgebend. Wir können höchstens hinzufügen, daß No. 4 ursprünglich Notturno und No. 7 Intermezzo benannt war.

DREI INTERMEZZI FÜR PIANOFORTE.
Op. 117.

VORLAGEN:

1. Die Original-Handschrift des Komponisten im Besitz der Gesellschaft der Musikfreunde in Wien. Sechs Blätter zwölfzeiligen Klavier-Notenpapiers in Hochformat ohne Überschrift, Namenszug und Datum.

Wien, im Frühjahr 1927.

2. Des Komponisten Handexemplar der ersten Ausgabe in demselben Besitz. Diese Ausgabe erschien unter dem Titel »Drei Intermezzi für Pianoforte von Johannes Brahms. Op. 117. No. 1. No. 2. No. 3. Verlag und Eigenthum für alle Länder von N. Simrock in Berlin. 1892.« Verlagsnummer 9876.

BEMERKUNGEN:

Im Handexemplar hat Brahms nachträglich noch einige unwesentliche Stichfehler korrigiert. Sonst ist die erste Ausgabe tadellos und war für uns maßgebend. Sie stimmt auch mit der Handschrift, obwohl diese nicht Stichvorlage war, vollständig überein, bis auf folgende Kleinigkeiten: Seite 4 (132) lautet in der Handschrift die Tempobezeichnung einfach Andante con moto. Seite (133) 5, Takt 3 ist, genau in der Mitte des Taktes, vor Eintritt des *p*, als Ergebnis des *rit.* — — — durch freistehende ⌢ in beiden Systemen eine »Luftpause« angedeutet, die die beiden Teile des Stücks (B moll und Des dur) auseinanderhält. Seite 6 (134), Takt 1 ist für die letzte Note der rechten Hand als Ergebnis des ——— ein *f* vorgeschrieben, worauf auch gleich das *p* des nächsten Taktes fällt. Daß Seite 6 (134), Zeile 4, Takt 2 die drittletzte Note der rechten Hand in der Handschrift ein c^2 ist, ist gewiß nur ein Schreibfehler; ebenso Seite (135) 7, wo im drittletzten Takt die erste Note der linken Hand in der Handschrift eine Hilfslinie zu wenig hat und als Des_1 erscheint. Im folgenden, vorletzten Takt fehlen in der Handschrift noch die Noten für die linke Hand; das ist aber kein Schreibfehler. Seite (139) 11, Zeile 3, Takt 3 lauten die aneinander gebundenen Noten für den Daumen der linken Hand in der Handschrift *e* (nicht *d*). Die Stelle Seite 12 (140), Takte 9—11 hatte Brahms ursprünglich so geformt, wie Seite (137) 9, Takt 9 und 10; als das Stück fertig war, änderte er sie zuerst so:

dann, noch in der Handschrift, wie sie im Druck steht.

KLAVIERSTÜCKE. Op. 118 und 119.

VORLAGE:

Des Komponisten Handexemplar der ersten Ausgabe im Besitz der Gesellschaft der Musikfreunde in Wien. Diese Ausgabe erschien unter dem Titel »Clavierstücke von Johannes Brahms. op. 118. No. 1. Intermezzo, A moll. No. 2. Intermezzo, A dur. No. 3. Ballade, G moll. No. 4. Intermezzo, F moll. No. 5. Romanze, F dur. No. 6. Intermezzo, Es moll. op. 119. No. 1. Intermezzo, H moll. No. 2. Intermezzo, E moll. No. 3. Intermezzo, C dur. No. 4. Rhapsodie, Es dur. Verlag und Eigenthum für alle Länder von N. Simrock in Berlin. 1893.« Zwei Hefte. Verlagsnummern 10054 und 10055.

BEMERKUNG:

Das Handexemplar weist keine nachträglichen Veränderungen von Brahms auf und war bei seiner großen Korrektheit maßgebend. Zum Unterschied der beiden Hefte geben wir im Kopftitel die Zahl der Stücke an.

Eusebius Mandyczewski.

Scherzo
für Pianoforte

Seinem Freunde Ernst Ferdinand Wenzel zugeeignet

Johannes Brahms, Op.4
(Veröffentlicht 1854)

Rasch und feurig

Da capo lo Scherzo senza repetizio_
ne sin al segno ⊕ e poi Trio II.

Trio II
Molto espressivo

Balladen
für Pianoforte

Julius O. Grimm gewidmet

Johannes Brahms, Op.10
(Veröffentlicht 1856)

1

Nach der schottischen Ballade: „Edward" in Herders „Stimmen der Völker"

J. B. 60

2

Molto staccato e leggiero

3
Intermezzo

4

Andante con moto

Più lento
Col intimissimo sentimento ma senza troppo marcare la Melodia

Walzer
für Pianoforte

Dr. Eduard Hanslick zugeeignet

Johannes Brahms, Op. 39
(Veröffentlicht 1867)

Poco sostenuto

4

Poco più Andante

7

12

15

16

Walzer
für Pianoforte

Dr Eduard Hanslick zugeeignet

Erleichterte Ausgabe

Johannes Brahms, Op.39
(Veröffentlicht 1867)

Tempo giusto

J. B. 61ª

Poco sostenuto

4

Poco più Andante

7

15

16

Acht Klavierstücke

Johannes Brahms, Op. 76
(Veröffentlicht 1879)

1. Capriccio

2. Capriccio

3. Intermezzo

4. Intermezzo

5. Capriccio

Agitato, ma non troppo presto
Sehr aufgeregt, doch nicht zu schnell

6. Intermezzo

7. Intermezzo

Moderato semplice

8. Capriccio

Grazioso ed un poco vivace
Anmutig lebhaft

Zwei Rhapsodien

für Pianoforte

Frau Elisabeth von Herzogenberg gewidmet

1

Johannes Brahms, Op. 79
(Veröffentlicht 1880)

in tempo

2

Molto passionato, ma non troppo allegro.

Fantasien
für Pianoforte

Johannes Brahms, Op. 116
(Veröffentlicht 1892)

1. Capriccio

2. Intermezzo

3. Capriccio

Un poco meno Allegro

4. Intermezzo

5. Intermezzo

Andante con grazia ed intimissimo sentimento

6. Intermezzo

7. Capriccio

Drei Intermezzi
für Pianoforte

Johannes Brahms, Op. 117
(Veröffentlicht 1892)

1

Schlaf sanft mein Kind, schlaf sanft und schön!
Mich dauert's sehr, dich weinen sehn.
(Schottisch. Aus Herders Volksliedern)

Più Adagio

pp sempre ma molto espressivo

Un poco più Andante

2

Andante non troppo e con molto espressione

3

Andante con moto

Più moto ed espressivo

dolce ma espress.

Sechs Klavierstücke

Johannes Brahms, Op. 118
(Veröffentlicht 1893)

1. Intermezzo

Allegro non assai, ma molto appassionato

2. Intermezzo

Andante teneramente

3. Ballade

Allegro energico

4. Intermezzo

Allegretto un poco agitato

5. Romanze

Allegretto grazioso

molto p e dolce sempre

p dolce

p leggiero

6. Intermezzo

Andante, largo e mesto

Vier Klavierstücke

Johannes Brahms, Op. 119
(Veröffentlicht 1893)

1. Intermezzo

2. Intermezzo

Andantino un poco agitato

3. Intermezzo

4. Rhapsodie

Allegro risoluto